Financial Strategies for Corporate Executives

A Handbook

Christopher B. Walling

ISBN 978-0-557-09537-7

Contents

Chapter 4

Company/Shareholder Policies

Chapter 5

Estate Planning for Corporate Executives

Chapter 6

Career Transition

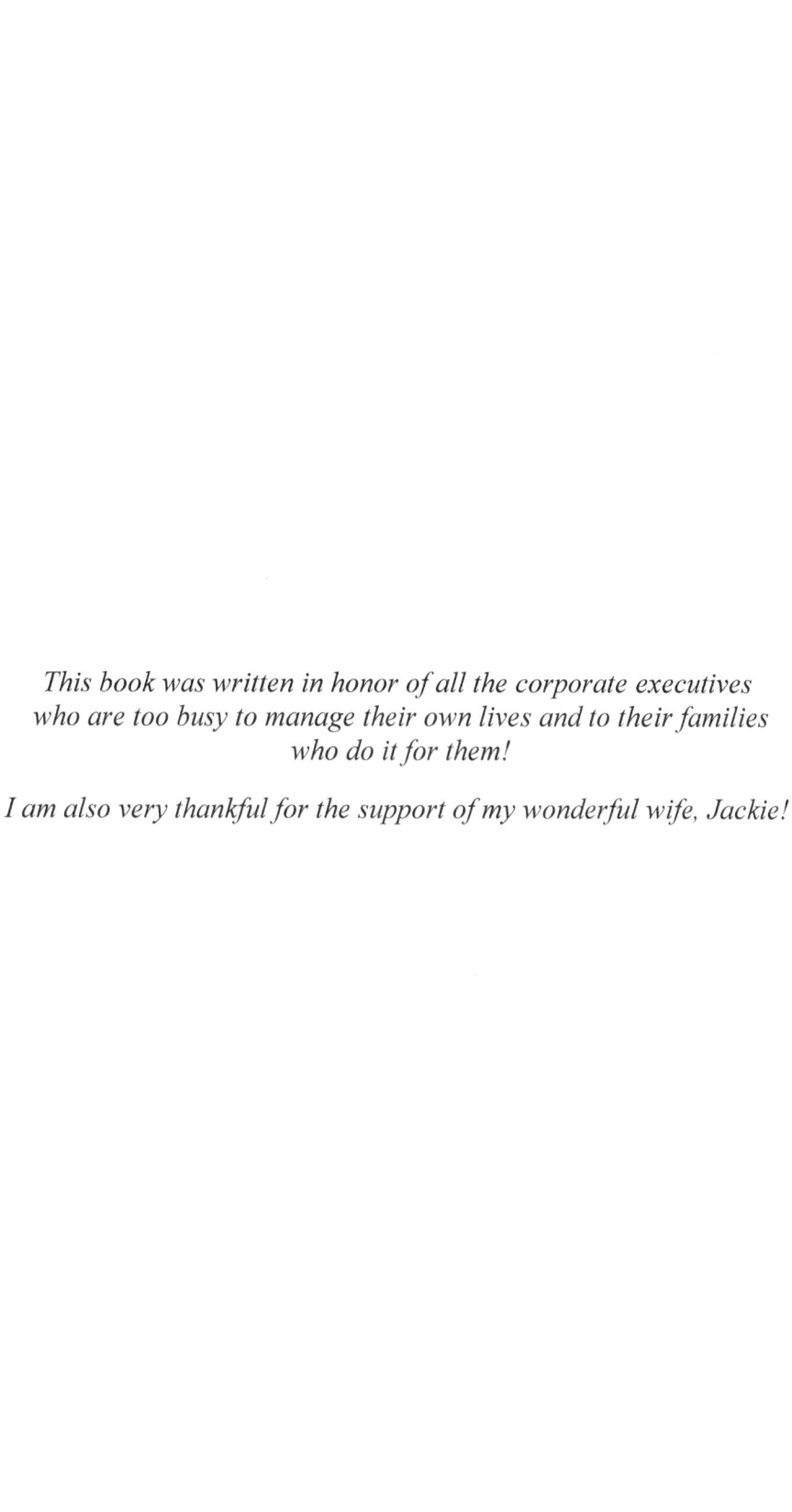

This book was written in honor of all the corporate executives who are too busy to manage their own lives and to their families who do it for them!

I am also very thankful for the support of my wonderful wife, Jackie!

Preface

My goal in writing this handbook is to help corporate executives have a basic understanding of financial terms and strategies to help them be successful in their financial life. Being a corporate executive takes endurance and stamina. After the business day is done, energy and patience is needed to follow through on outside activities and leaves little time for taking care of personal financial planning. Many corporate executives use a financial planner, or advisor to help them with the basics of their money, but very few executives sit down with advisors to get educated on other financial strategies that they should really know.

In my experience as a corporate executive, as well as working with clients, friends and relatives who are corporate executives, I am surprised how few resources are available to teach us about executive compensation and options. This handbook only scratches the surface, but I hope it will help you ask better questions when looking for or leaving a job; as well as help you work with your own advisors and expand your discussion to help preserve and manage wealth.

Regardless of how long you have been an executive, I hope this book will help you understand and communicate better with your human resources department as well as with other executives. I also hope that some of these strategies will introduce you to ample number of strategies that can help you sleep better at night; when it comes to your company stock and stock options.

It is a complex world and the fluid lifestyle of corporate executives has shifted from job security to job uncertainty and it is time to take more control of your financial life and realize that nothing lasts for ever.

Enjoy!

Chris Walling Powell, Ohio May 2009

Disclaimers

Options

Options Involve risk and are not suitable for all investors. For information on the uses and risks of options you can obtain a copy of "Characteristics and Risks of Standardized Options" from the Options Clearing Corporation. Copies of this document may be obtained from your broker, from any exchange on which options are traded or by contacting The Options Clearing Corporation, One North Wacker Dr., Suite 500, Chicago, IL 60606 (1-800-678-4667).

Borrowing against Securities

Borrowing against securities may not be suitable for everyone. If the securities decline in the market value below the borrowers maintenance level the borrower may be required to pay down the loan or deposit additional securities as collateral. If the borrower cannot do so, all or a portion of the collateral may be liquidated and a potential taxable event may occur. Please contact your legal or tax advisor with respect to these types of loans against securities.

Tax or legal advice

This book and its materials and any tax related statements are not intended or written to be used, and cannot be used or relied upon, by any such taxpayer for the purpose of avoiding tax penalties. Any taxpayer should seek advice based upon the taxpayer's particular circumstances from an independent tax advisor.

Chapter 1

Compensation and Benefits

Executive Life Insurance

Although the life insurance benefits that many corporations offer to their employees through group term plans are efficient in providing benefits to currently active non-executives, group term life insurance has several shortcomings in providing executive life insurance coverage, including:

Disproportionately high tax cost to the executive for the coverage provided

Limitations on coverage amounts

Very high cost to the company to provide necessary post-retirement coverage

Lack of portability upon termination or retirement

Lack of flexibility to meet estate-planning needs.

Therefore, it is necessary to introduce a few life insurance concepts that are still applicable today for corporate executives.

Term Insurance Carve Out

- Premiums paid under a Group Term Insurance Plan for all employees are deductible up to $50,000 death benefit

- Premiums paid for individual Term Policies are generally not deductible

- However, a portion of premiums under Treasury Regulation Section 1.79 allows for executives to be ""carved out"" to receive permanent life insurance coverage and a portion of the premiums will be tax deductible to the corporation. The remaining premium can be charged to employees in various ways.

Executive Bonus

A corporation pays the entire premium and charges it to the executive as compensation under IRS Section 162. The executive then only pays the income tax due on the transaction. The Executive owns the policy and names the beneficiary and it is portable for the executive to take if he leaves the company. The corporation has no control over the policy and is not used as a ""'golden handcuff''.

Split Dollar Purchases

Under traditional split dollar plans, the company recovers all premiums paid through a receipt of the portion of the death benefit or by receiving part of the cash value upon surrender. This type of split dollar is still a good choice in situations not subject to Sarbanes Oxley. Revenue ruling 2002-8 changed all the rules and made ""'equity"'" split dollar not available. Adding further confusion, a provision of the Sarbanes-Oxley Act, signed into law in July, prohibits public companies from making loans to executive officers or directors. Because certain types of split-dollar arrangements might be characterized as loans, the act might eliminate such arrangements.

Split-dollar isn't used for all employees, because funding the policy sufficiently to recover the company's costs requires significantly greater cash flow than group insurance. Although the long-term economics of split-dollar are more attractive, the appetite for cash flow is typically a consideration when deciding how many executives to include in such a program.

Nonqualified Deferred Compensation

A nonqualified deferred compensation plan is an arrangement that allows an employee to defer payment of compensation to a future date. A nonqualified deferred compensation plan is not subject to the tax-qualified retirement plan limitations and is exempt from many of the rules of the Employee Retirement Income Security Act of 1974(ERISA). Under a nonqualified deferred compensation plan, the employee merely holds an unfunded and unsecured promise from the company to make future compensation payments to the employee.

Advantages of Nonqualified Deferred Compensation Plan

For Executives	For the Company
* Provides for the deferral of taxes	Aids in recruitment and retention
* Restores benefits lost due to 401(k) limits	Rewards executives for length of service and performance
* Supplements retirement income	Provides a cost effective plan that could have favorable financial impact

* Provides a financial planning vehicle using pre-tax dollars

Other Types of Nonqualified Plans

Supplemental Executive Retirement Plan (SERP)

-A SERP is a plan that provides enhanced retirement benefits for executives. Usually, no employee contributions are required under a SERP. The plan benefits can be in addition to or offset by benefits from a tax qualified plan. A SERP generally targets certain income-replacement ratios and is structured as a defined benefit plan.

Excess Benefit Plan

-An ERISA excess benefit plan is ""a plan maintained by an employer solely for the purpose of providing benefits for certain employees in excess of the code section 415 limitations on contributions and benefits.""

An example:

* A company qualified defined contribution retirement plan provides annual contributions equal to 20 percent of an employee's compensation for the year, subject to the qualified plan annual contribution limit. For a Vice President,

who has an annual salary of $300,000, that potential contribution would come to $60,000 (.2 x $300,000). In 2007, however, only $45,000 can be added to his qualified retirement plan account because that is the limit for the year.

* Fortunately for this executive, his employer credits the remainder of the contribution ($15,000) to a nonqualified deferred compensation account, these credits earnings credits and losses as if the account were invested in the qualified plan, and pays out to his account when the qualified plan benefits are paid.

Executive Healthcare Insurance

Aside from the basic type of insurance available from employers, for your health insurance coverage there are also some excellent facilities that provide wellness testing and executive physical exams.

Nearly half of larger U.S. employers currently offer executive exam programs, according to a recent Arthur Andersen, Financial Executives Institute study. Forty eight percent of companies surveyed offer executive physicals as one their top ten executive perks - ranking second just behind cell phones (66%) and ahead of company cars (44%).

Despite its continued prevalence, new executive examination programs are not at the top of the priority list for many corporations today. It is a benefit that is alive and well, expected by many senior executives, yet rarely introduced as a new benefit.

Paid for Financial Planning and Other Perks

Companies say they need to offer ample benefits to attract and retain top-flight shelf managers. Other perks, such as the personal use of corporate jets, company provided chauffeurs and company-paid financial planning, can add tens of thousands of dollars to an executive's total compensation. Just make sure that the financial planning groups that you use have the best incentive to help you with your planning, not just to sell you additional products or services.

Long Term Care Insurance

Research shows that at least 70 percent of people over age 65 will require some long-term care services at some point in their lives! (Department of Health and Human Services, National Clearinghouse for Long-Term Care Information, September 2008.)

Additionally, the cost of long-term care services may be surprising. That's why it's such a good idea to consider long-term care insurance as an integral part of a well-rounded financial plan. It may help protect your hard-earned assets, and provide more control over how and where you receive care should you need it.

Long-term care (LTC) is the assistance that is provided to people who are unable to perform the Activities of Daily Living (ADLs) that healthy, fully functional people do independently and on a daily basis.

The need for long-term care services arises from chronic health conditions and/or physical disabilities - such as a stroke, Multiple Sclerosis, Parkinson's or Alzheimer's disease, and are provided over a long period of time.

Some people mistakenly assume that most people receive long-term care services in nursing homes. In actuality, a number of people in need of long-term care services receive them at an assisted living facility or in one's own home.

The best time for Corporate Executives to purchase long term care is when they are young and it good health and in most cases, policies can be purchased with a spouse with a number of discounts.

Disability Insurance

When you're healthy and working, it's hard to imagine being disabled by illness or injury. A corporate executive's biggest risk is loss of income and most company group disability plans only do not cover full income replacement.

One in 3 three working Americans will become disabled for 90 days or more before the age 65.[*]

    • •   The average disability absence is two and a half years.[*]

•• More than 80% of working Americans don't have disability income insurance or aren't covered adequately. **

Why you can sleep better at night with disability insurance:

* Social Security disability payments are limited to disabilities expected to last at least 12 months or end in death. To qualify, you must be unable to engage in any type of work.
* Personal Savings can best be used to build a comfortable future. Add up your monthly bills, then multiply by 12 and you can see how fast even substantial savings can be depleted due to unexpected illness or injury.
* Long- Term Disability Insurance offered through your employer is a start. But workplace disability benefits often times cover only about 50% of your income. Can your family survive on half of a paycheck?
* Group LTD usually covers only a portion of an employee's compensation
* LTD benefits are generally taxable if the employer pays the premiums.
* Many plans don't cover bonus or incentive compensation and there is often a maximum monthly cap and, as a result, an employee's monthly after-tax income during a disability may drop by 50% or more!
* Many plans don't cover bonus or incentive compensation and there is often a maximum monthly cap and, as a result, an employee's monthly after-tax income during a disability may drop by 50% or more!

* Commissioner's Individual Disability Table A
** National Underwriter Magazine, May 2001

Directors and Officer Liability Insurance

This is insurance payable to the directors and officers of a company, or to the corporation itself, to cover damages or defense costs in the event they are sued for wrongful acts while they were with that company. The company itself usually purchases D&O insurance, even when it is for the sole benefit of directors and officers. Reasons for doing so are many, but most commonly would assist a company in attracting and retaining directors.

Chapter 2

Stock Option Planning

Stock Option Planning

Stock option planning is one of the most important areas for corporate executives to understand, as a significant amount of wealth can be in the form of options. There also tends to be concerns with liquidity, leverage, and concentration risk that must also be addressed. The goal for corporate executives and their stock options should be to understand;

* What type of options do I have and how do I exercise these options?

* How to convert options that are ripe for selling without overpaying income tax

* How to manage options positions without giving up value or overexposure to risk

* Estate planning strategies and gifting strategies for stock options

Exercising Stock Options

Exercise and Hold

An exercise and hold strategy means that you purchase the stock at the exercise price and continue to hold the stock after exercise. The stock is not sold, which means you use out of pocket funds to cover the purchase price as well as any taxes or fees.

Exercise and Sell- To-Cover

An exercise and sell-to-cover involves buying stock at the exercise price and selling only enough shares to cover the cost of the stock, plus fees and taxes. With this strategy, no out of pocket money is required and the remaining shares not sold to cover the option are held or deposited in your account.

Exercise and Sell All

Exercise and sell all options refers to the simultaneous exercise of an option and sale of all shares of stock at the current market price. You will receive cash in the amount of the difference between the market price and exercise price minus any taxes or fees.

Hold Options and Do Nothing

You may always choose to hold options and do nothing because your options may be exercised any time up to expiration date. This is a strategy if your options are under water, or out of the money or you do not want to pay taxes in a certain year.

Stock Option Holding Requirements

The holding period refers to the length of time the stock needs to be held after exercise. Some stock options may stipulate required holding periods, but by law the long-term gain capital treatment for Incentive Stock Options (ISO) is two years from the date of grant and one year from the date of exercise. Exercise prior to these dates could trigger the loss of preferential tax treatment.

Other Options Strategies and Gifting

Reload of Options

Certain companies allow employees the ability to fund an option exercise with stock they already own and then the company automatically awards a new option. Sometimes this option is called a replacement option, restoration option or reload option.

Stock Swap

A stock swap is another exercise strategy that allows option holders to exercise stock options without paying cash. Stock that is currently held at the company is used as payment for the exercise of the stock option. In most cases, no tax is due on the swap but may be due on shares received and this can be a great alternative form of funding.

Gifting Stock Options

Stock options are a large part of a corporate executive's net worth and there can be key benefits to financial and estate planning that comes from gifting stock options. It is very important to talk with your plan administrator to ask if options are transferable.

* Gifting employee stock options may reduce transfer taxes and estate taxes at death, but is irrevocable and cannot be reversed

* After gifting any appreciation escapes estate tax

* Once heirs exercise Non-qualified options, income tax will be due to the donor based upon the difference of current stock price and exercise price

* The annual gift tax exclusion and estate tax exclusion should be reviewed and observed.

Non-Qualified Stock Options (NQSO)

Non-qualified stock options result in additional taxable income to the recipient at the time that they are exercised, the amount being the difference between the exercise price and the market value on that date.

Non-qualified stock options are frequently preferred by employers because the issuer is allowed to take a tax deduction equal to the amount the recipient is required to include in his or her income.

Incentive Stock Options (ISO)

Incentive stock options (ISO's), are a type of employee stock option that can be granted only to employees and confer a tax benefit. ISO's are also sometimes referred to as incentive share options or Qualified Stock Options.

The tax benefit is that on exercise the individual does not have to pay ordinary tax (nor employment taxes) on the difference between the exercise price and the fair market value of the shares issued (however, the holder may have to pay U.S. alternative minimum tax instead). Instead, if the shares are held for 1 year from the date of exercise and 2 years from the date of grant, then the profit (if any) made on sale of the shares is taxed as long-term capital gain. Long-term capital gain is taxed in the U.S. at lower rates than ordinary income.

Although ISOs have more favorable tax treatment than non- ISO's (aka non-statutory stock option (NSO) or non-qualified stock option (NQSO)), they also require the holder to take on more risk by having to hold onto the stock for a longer period of time in order to receive the better tax treatment.

Chapter 3

Portfolio Diversification and Monetization

Stock Options Strategies for Insurance and Hedging

Most strategies that options investors use have limited risk but also limited profit potential. For this reason, options strategies are not get-rich-quick schemes. Transactions generally require less capital than equivalent stock transactions, and therefore return smaller dollar figures - but a potentially greater percentage of the investment - than equivalent stock transactions.

Even those investors who use options in speculative strategies, such as writing uncovered calls, don't usually realize dramatic returns. The potential profit is limited to the premium received for the contract, and the potential loss is often unlimited. While leverage means the percentage returns can be significant, here, too, the amount of cash changing hands is smaller than with equivalent stock transactions.

Although options may not be appropriate for everyone, they're among the most flexible of investment choices. Depending on the contract, options can protect or enhance the portfolios of many different kinds of investors in rising, falling, and neutral markets.

Reducing Your Risk

For many investors, options are useful as tools of risk management, acting as insurance policies against a drop in stock prices. For example, if an investor is concerned that the price of his shares in LMN Corporation is about to drop, he can purchase puts that give him the right to sell his stock at the strike price, no matter how low the market price drops before expiration. At the cost of the option's premium, the investor has insured himself against losses below the strike price. This type of option practice is also known as hedging. While hedging with options may help you manage risk, it's important to remember that all investments carry some risk, and returns are never guaranteed. Investors who use options to manage risk look for ways to limit potential loss. They may choose to purchase options, since loss is limited to the price paid for the premium. In return, they gain the right to buy or sell the underlying security at an acceptable price for them. They can also profit from a rise in the value of the option's premium, if they choose to sell it back to the market rather than exercise it. Since writers of options are sometimes forced into buying or selling stock at an unfavorable price, the risk associated with certain short positions may be higher.

Many options strategies are designed to minimize risk by hedging existing portfolios. While options can act as safety nets, they're not risk free. Since transactions usually open and close in the short term, gains can be realized very quickly. This means that losses can mount quickly as well. It's important to understand all the risks associated with holding, writing, and trading options before you include them in your investment portfolio.

Risking Your Principal

Like other securities - including stocks, bonds, and mutual funds - options carry no guarantees, and you must be aware that it's possible to lose all of the principal you invest, and sometimes more. As an options holder, you risk the entire amount of the premium you pay. But as an options writer, you take on a much higher level of risk. For example, if you write an uncovered call, you face unlimited potential loss, since there is no cap on how high a stock price can rise. However, since initial options investments usually requires less capital than equivalent stock positions, your potential cash losses as an options investor are usually smaller than if you'd bought the underlying stock or sold the stock short. The exception to this general rule occurs when you use options to provide leverage: Percentage returns are often high, but it's important to remember that percentage losses can be high as well.

Options Involve risk and are not suitable for all investors. For information on the uses and risks of options you can obtain a copy of ""Characteristics and Risks of Standardized Options"" from the Options Clearing Corporation. Copies of this document may be obtained from your broker, from any exchange on which options are traded or by contacting The Options Clearing Corporation, One North Wacker Dr., Suite 500, Chicago, IL 60606 (1-80   0-678-4667).

83(b) Election

Under Section 83 of the Internal Revenue Code, the corporate executive would not recognize income (the difference between fair market value and the price paid) until the stock vests. However, if an executive makes a voluntary Section 83(b) election, the executive recognizes ""income"" upon the purchase of the stock.

Typically, the purchase price for the stock and the fair market value are the same. Therefore, if an 83(b) election is made, there is no income recognized. Thus, an executive should almost always make an 83(b) election. The benefits of an 83(b) election generally are starting the one year capital gain holding period and freezing ordinary income (or alternative minimum tax) recognition to the purchase date.

If the executive does not make the 83(b) election, then he or she may have income at the stock ""vests."" The income will be substantial if the value of the shares increases substantially over time.

Why Doesn't Everyone Make an 83(b) Election?

- Employee must have the cash to cover the taxes due

- If employee leaves company before vesting, she could lose the restricted stock

- If the stock prices falls rather than rises, the executive could pay more in taxes than by not making the election.

Corporate Executive Blind Trust

Corporate Executives and insiders who own millions of shares in their companies typically enjoy a very substantial net worth. But with that net worth comes in a single company stock there is tremendous downside risk. Selling those shares of company stock to achieve diversification and reduce risk is not easy, since federal regulations govern when insiders can sell stock.

There is, however, a solution to this problem - the blind trust. This strategy enables an insider to give a trustee the sole responsibility to decide on the timing of sales of company stock, without participation by, or knowledge of, the insider. Hence, insiders can achieve diversification, over time, without running afoul of securities regulations.

Benefits

* Provides protection from the appearance of improperly selling of company stock

* Provides protection from claims of using insider information

* Potential Estate and Financial planning vehicle

* Appoints a separate fiduciary with broad investment objectives

* May reduce paperwork burden of regulatory filings and trading restrictions

Risks

* Voting rights are not retained by Corporate Executive or grantor

* Grantor cannot have investment control over timing or number of shares sold

* Grantor has limited ability to communicate with Trustee

Rule 10b-18 Buyback Plan

Technically, SEC (Securities Exchange Commission) Rule 10b-18 provides a safe harbor only for repurchases of common stock. In practice, it is often used as a guideline for repurchases of other securities as well.

Even though compliance with Rule 10b-18 isn't mandatory, it does reduce the potential for error in executing a buyback.

Specifics of Rule 10b-18

* The company repurchasing shares may not use more than one broker to acquire the shares per each day

* A repurchase may not be the first trade of the day. Repurchases may not be made in the last ten minutes of the trading day. These rules do not apply to over-the-counter securities.

* A repurchase may not be bid at a price higher than the highest independent bid or last price of the last trade.

Repurchases per day may not exceed 25% of the average daily volume of the previous 4 calendar weeks. Block purchases not affected by a broker-dealer are excluded from this restriction.

Rule 10b5-1 Trading Plans

Sec Rule I0b5-1, allows directors, officers and other executives with access to material nonpublic information about their company and its securities to enter into a pre-established written trading plan. This provides an ""affirmative defense"" against any allegation of insider trading.

Key Benefits

* Allows for sale of company stock on your own schedule, enabling you to diversify a concentrated portfolio

* Provides you an affirmative defense against insider trading allegations

* Enables a pre-established buying or selling program for specified time frames and at specific limit or market prices

* Mitigates how sales might signal the market

* Enables you to buy or sell stock during blackout periods that are subject to company approval

* May reduce administrative burdens regarding approval of insider purchases and sales by general counsel

Alternative Investments and Hedge Funds

As a corporate executive with respectable compensation there are many investment opportunities that are available and one of the fastest growing areas is hedge funds and alternative investments, such as real estate and private equity.

This asset class has been designed to enhance investors overall portfolio return while also reducing risk. There are many funds available around the world and it is important to work with an advisor who understands your goal and objectives as well of the landscape of alternative investments.

By using a fund of funds of private equity or hedge funds executives can gain access to leading money managers from around the world and also take advantage of diversification in an industry that has a more limited transparency than traditional investments.

Various Types of Hedge Funds

Distressed Securities: Buys equity, debt, or trade claims at deep discounts of companies in or facing bankruptcy or reorganization. These funds can profit from the market's lack of understanding of the true value of the deeply discounted securities and because the majority of institutional investors cannot own below investment grade securities. (This selling pressure creates the deep discount.) Results generally not dependent on the direction of the markets.

Emerging Markets: Invests in equity or debt of emerging (less mature) markets that tend to have higher inflation and volatile growth. Short selling is not permitted in many emerging markets, and, therefore, effective hedging is often not available, although Brady debt can be partially hedged via U.S. Treasury futures and currency markets.

Funds of Hedge Funds: Mix and match hedge funds and other pooled investment vehicles. This blending of different strategies and asset classes aims to provide a more stable long-term investment return than any of the individual funds. Returns, risk, and volatility can be controlled by the mix of underlying strategies and funds the mix of underlying strategies and funds can control returns, risk, and volatility. Capital preservation is generally an important consideration. Volatility depends on the mix and ratio of strategies employed.

Income: Invests with primary focus on yield or current income rather than solely on capital gains. May utilize leverage to buy bonds and sometimes fixed income derivatives in order to profit from principal appreciation and interest income.

Macro: Aims to profit from changes in global economies, typically brought about by shifts in government policy that impact interest rates, in turn affecting currency, stock, and bond markets. Macro hedge fund strategies can Participates invest in all major markets -- —equities, bonds, currencies and commodities -- —though not always at the same time. Uses leverage and derivatives to accentuate the impact of market moves. Utilizes hedging, but the leveraged directional investments tend to make the largest impact on performance.

Market Neutral - Arbitrage: Attempts to hedge out most market risk by taking offsetting positions, often in different securities of the same issuer. For example, arbitrage funds can be long convertible bonds and short the underlying issuer's equity.   These funds focus on obtaining returns with low or no correlation to both the equity and bond markets. These relative value strategies include fixed income arbitrage, mortgage backed securities, capital structure arbitrage, and closed-end fund arbitrage.

Market Neutral- Securities Hedging: Invests equally in long and short equity portfolios generally in the same sectors of the market. Market risk is greatly reduced, but effective stock analysis and stock picking is essential to obtaining meaningful results. Leverage may be used to enhance returns. Sometimes uses market index futures to hedge out systematic (market) risk. Relative benchmark index usually T -bills.

Market Timing: Allocates assets among different asset classes depending on the manager's view of the economic or market outlook. Portfolio emphasis may swing widely between asset classes. Unpredictability of market movements and the difficulty of timing entry and exit from markets add to the volatility of this strategy.

Opportunistic: Investment theme changes from strategy to strategy as opportunities arise to profit from events such as IPO's, sudden price changes often caused by an interim earnings disappointment, hostile bids, and other event-driven opportunities. May utilize several of these investing styles at a given time and is not restricted to any particular investment approach or asset class.

Multi Strategy: Investment approach is diversified by employing various strategies simultaneously to realize short and long-term gains. Other strategies may include systems trading such as trend following and various diversified technical strategies. This style of investing allows the manager to overweight or underweight different strategies to best capitalize on current investment opportunities.

Short Selling: Sells securities short in anticipation of being able to buy them back at a future date at a lower price due to the manager's assessment of the overvaluation of the securities, or the market, or in anticipation of earnings disappointments often due to accounting irregularities, new competition, change of management, etc. Often used as a hedge to offset long-only portfolios and by those who feel the market is approaching a bearish cycle. High risk.

Special Situations: Invests in event-driven situations such as mergers, hostile takeovers, reorganizations, or leveraged buyouts. Special situation hedge funds may involve simultaneous purchase of stock in companies being acquired, and the sale of stock in its acquirer, hoping to profit from the spread between the current market price and the ultimate purchase price of the company. This strategy may also utilize derivatives to leverage returns and to hedge out interest rate and/or market risk. Results generally not dependent on direction of market

Value: Invests in securities perceived to be selling at deep discounts to their intrinsic or potential worth. Such securities may be out of favor or under followed by analysts. Long-term holding, patience, and strong discipline are often required until the ultimate value is recognized by the market recognizes the ultimate value.

Ask your advisor about these funds but do your homework and make sure you understand how long you need to stay invested to get a decent rate of return.

Chapter 4

Company/Shareholder Policies

Insider Trading

Insider trading is the trading of a corporations stock or other securities (e.g. bonds or stock options) by individuals with potential access to non-public information about the company. In most countries, trading by corporate insiders such as officers; key employees, directors, and large shareholders may be legal, if this trading is done in a way that does not take advantage of non-public information. However, the term is frequently used to refer to a practice in which an insider or a related party trades on non-public information obtained during the performance of the insider's duties at the corporation, or otherwise in breach of a fiduciary duty or other relationship of trust and confidence or where the non-public information was misappropriated from the company.

In the United States and several other jurisdictions, trading conducted by corporate officers, key employees, directors, or significant shareholders (in the U.S., defined as beneficial owners often percent or more of the firm's equity securities) must be reported to the regulator or publicly disclosed, usually within a few business days of the trade. Many investors follow the summaries of these insider trades in the hope that mimicking these trades will be profitable. While ""legal"" insider trading cannot be based on material non-public information, some investors believe corporate insiders nonetheless may have better insights into the health of a corporation (broadly speaking) and that their trades otherwise convey important information (e.g., about the pending retirement of an important officer selling shares, greater commitment to the corporation by officers purchasing shares, etc.)

Illegal insider trading is believed to raise the cost of capital for securities issuers, thus decreasing overall economic growth.

Trading Windows

Trading Windows are periods of predetermined time when corporate executives subject to insider trading rules can sell their stock with legal approval. Regulation contemplates three types of written plans, any of which is sufficient to invoke the safe harbor protection: (i) a document specifying that particular trades will occur at specified prices, on specified dates, for specified numbers of shares; (ii) a document specifying a formula pursuant to which trades will occur; or (iii) a document granting an outsider complete discretion to make the trades, without access to any material nonpublic information about the company.

Right of First Refusal

Right of first refusal (ROFR or RFR) is a contractual right that gives its holder the option to enter a business transaction with the owner of something, according to specified terms, before the owner is entitled to enter into that transaction with a third party. In brief, the right of first refusal is similar in concept to a call option.

Registration Rights for Restricted Stock

Registration rights entitle investors to force a company to register shares of common stock issuable upon conversion of preferred stock with the Securities and Exchange Commission.

Federal and state securities laws place certain limitations on the transfer of shares that have not been registered. Rule 144 of the Securities Act of 1933 requires that securities be held for at least one year before being sold. Among other things, Rule 144 also requires that certain current public information about the company be available and limits the volume of shares that can be sold, unless the seller has held the securities for at least two years and is not an affiliate of the company. Registration allows venture funds to freely sell the shares without complying with these restrictions even if they are deemed affiliates due to significant shareholdings or a director on the board.

Registration involves filing a registration statement with the SEC, which is an expensive and time consuming process. As a practical matter, registration rights are rarely used and have little practical effect on a company until after an initial public offering (IPO). However, some venture funds and attorneys seem to spend a long time negotiating these provisions, when they have little practical impact. Registration rights are negotiated between the company and the investors, well before underwriters are involved. At the time of an IPO and subsequent underwritten public offerings, underwriters will have the ability to dictate whether investors are allowed to sell, which makes the registration rights negotiated at the time of the venture financing a mere starting point for discussions with the company and the underwriters.

Pledging Shares

This is a situation where an investor can pledge shares of stocks as collateral security to secure the payment of debt. The "Pledgee" may assign or transfer debt and the collateral pledged to a third party such as a bank. Upon payment of the obligation for which the shares were pledged, the shares shall be returned to the original owner "Pledgor" and the pledge agreement shall be terminated. The stock pledge agreement grants a security interest in specific shares of stock held by the shareholder in order to secure the shareholder's responsibility and commitment. This practice is typically used by companies that issue shares in exchange for promissory notes. Companies that issue shares in exchange for promissory notes typically use this practice.

Lock Up Agreements

A lock up agreement is a legally binding contract between the underwriters and insiders of a company prohibiting these individuals from selling any shares of stock for a specified period of time. Lock-up periods typically last 180 days (six months) but can on occasion last for as little as 120 days or as long as 365 days (one year).

Underwriters will have company executives, managers, employees and venture capitalists sign lock-up agreements to ensure an element of stability in the stock's price in the first few months of trading. When lock-ups expire, restricted people are permitted to sell their stock, which sometimes (if these insiders are looking to sell their stock) results in a drastic drop in share price due to the huge increase in supply of stock.

Restricted Stock

Restricted Stock is stock that was not acquired in registered sale. It is generally acquired from a company in a private transaction or as compensation. If you have restricted stock~ it will usually have a ""legend"" stamped on the stock certificate indicating that the stock is not registered for public sale.

Depending on the restrictions or rules of sale for company stock there is a chance that loans can be made against restricted stock to help an executive generate additional cash flow. There are also times when restricted stock can be hedged using options or the equivalent type of stock or industry to help reduce the risk of a downturn in a certain company or industry. This is an area to approach a good financial firm that has experience in provided loans and hedging for corporate executives.

Control Securities

Control stock is stock owned by people who directly or indirectly control the management of the issuer. This would usually be the senior officers, directors and large shareholders. Such people or entities may also be referred to as ""affiliates"". It is the security holder's ability to control the company, not how the stock was acquired that determines whether the stock is control securities. For example, a CFO of a company is considered an ""affiliate"" and may own control stock which stock, which has additional limitations and rules on sale and purchase.

Collateral Loans-What securities are eligible?

Restricted, control and concentrated stock of good quality will be considered eligible if they are saleable and margin-eligible (can loan against stock). Most securities registered on a national securities exchange or securities listed on the NASDAQ National Market System are eligible. Foreign securities with a liquid market, convertible bonds and other convertible securities are also eligible as long as available for margin.

When it comes to available credit on restricted stock or control stock, the amount depends on a few factors such as; the remaining holding period under rule 144, the number of shares outstanding and the stock daily trading volume. In most cases, you can borrow up to 50% of the market value of the stock or security and can use the loan to help diversify your overall holdings. There are numerous and changing regulatory rules for these types of loans so make sure to consult your advisors.

Chapter 5

Estate Planning for Corporate Executives

Estate planning can help you preserve your hard-earned assets and ensure that they go where you want them to go after you die. By planning your estate, you can save your family and heir's considerable time, expense, and grief by eliminating uncertainty about inheritance. Only by planning your estate *now* can you be ensure that all your wishes will be known and respected when you pass away.

The only way to pass on your entire estate without paying tax is by giving 100% of it to your spouse. When heirs other than a spouse receive assets from an estate, tax liabilities arise. There are five main types of taxes that your estate or your heirs may need to pay upon your death:

*   Federal estate taxes (also known as ""death taxes"")

*   State estate taxes –Taxes paid to state of residence

*   Capital gain taxes-Current capital gains due in that year

*   Inheritance taxes- Taxes for assets passed along to heirs

*   Income taxes-Current income taxes due for the current year

It's important to understand what these taxes are since you obviously will want to minimize the bite that taxes will take out of the estate you pass on to your heirs.

Wills and Trusts

Will: A will is a legal document in which you set out the rights and responsibilities of others for your property and minor children and/or disabled dependents in the event of your death. The best way to clarify misconceptions about what wills cover is by pointing out what wills do not cover. Wills *do not* direct what happens to:

1) **Personal property:**

Cars, boats, jewelry, clothes, and furniture. To direct personal property to specific heirs you'll likely have to prepare letters of instruction. Some states allow you to direct personal property to heirs in your will, so check your state's regulations to confirm.

2) Assets with named beneficiaries:

When you sign up for financial products, such as insurance, annuities, company pension plans, or individual retirement accounts (IRAs), you're asked to name a beneficiary for that policy. (You can change the beneficiary by contacting the company that issues the policy.)

3) Assets inside most trusts:

You don't legally own assets in a trust, so you can't will those assets

Living Wills

A living will is a document that states **in** advance the type of care that you would like to receive if you become terminally ill and can no longer express your wishes, such as after a stroke or catastrophic accident. Unlike durable medical powers of attorney, a living will provides guidance to medical personnel for specific situations but does *not* authorize a particular person to make decisions for you.

Please note that medical personnel are not *required* to follow the wishes outlined in your living will. To ensure that your medical care preferences are carried out, you need a durable medical power of attorney or a do not resuscitate order.

Do Not Resuscitate Orders (DNRs)

A do not resuscitate order (DNR) is a request *not* to have cardiopulmonary resuscitation (CPR) or any other heart-starting actions performed on you should your heart stop or you stop breathing. All states and medical personnel are required to honor these orders, though some refuse to on occasion. as DNRs inevitably result in death.

Letters of Instruction

A letter of instruction is a document that specifies to whom you would like to give personal property that's either not assigned to a beneficiary or not covered by your will. Letters of instruction typically do not cover every individual item you own. Instead, they apply to valuable objects not covered by wills, such as jewelry, coin collections, and so on.

Trusts

Trusts are legal entities used to protect various aspects of an estate. The most popular types of trusts are intended to shield significant assets, such as homes and other investments (stocks, bonds, etc.), from the costly process of probate. Trusts help dodge probate by actually ""owning"" your major assets: when you establish a trust, you must re-title the assets you are placing into the trust so that official ownership of those assets transfers from you to the trust. Trusts also have various other benefits. For example, trusts can:

* Protect information about your estate from public disclosure

* Protect life insurance from taxation, allowing it to be used to pay estate taxes Minimize estate and income taxes (assets in *charitable trusts* reduce taxes and generate tax deductions)

* Facilitate charitable giving and gifting to heirs.

All Trusts have **grantors, trustees**, and **beneficiaries**:

Grantors: The person or people who set up the trusts.

Trustees: The person, people, or entities (such as a bank trust department) that make decisions about investments, sales, and income distribution in the trust

Beneficiaries: The person, people, or entities that receive the benefits paid out by the trust (the grantor of the trust can specify the precise benefits that each of the beneficiaries will receive from the trust)

If you believe that a trust might be a valuable estate-planning tool for you, your best course of action is to read through the descriptions of different kinds of trusts and to discuss your needs with your financial advisor or a professional estate planner. Do not attempt to set up a trust by yourself.

Health and Education Exclusions

This type of trust can provide nearly perpetual deferral of generation skipping transfer (GST) taxes without allocation of the Generation Skipping Tax exemption. It incorporates philanthropic goals into an estate plan, enforces a focus on the purpose for which a trust distribution is being made, and favors distributions that enhance the education and health of a client's descendants. In addition, it provides significant creditor protection for the trust's beneficiaries; this is as close to an ironclad protection as one can get. The HEET also can act as a ready-made prenuptial agreement for every descendant into perpetuity. Yet this trust is not particularly aggressive or risky.

Gifting

Any person can gift money or assets to anyone they choose. Gifts are currently tax free up to specified annual and lifetime limits. Gifts are commonly used to:

* Pass money from one generation to the next Give money to organizations
* Provide financial aid to friends or relatives in need
* Set up educational savings plans

Gifts can also come in non-cash form, which can include personal property, free use of living quarters, and more.

Charitable giving is a way to "give back" to organizations that you feel could benefit from your financial assistance after you die. The government provides incentives to give to charity throughout your lifetime and via your estate after you die. These benefits include:

* Current tax deductions

* Significant reductions in capital gains and estate taxes due upon your death

Some of the best ways to add charitable giving to your estate planning strategy are:

* Donating assets

* Setting up charitable trusts

* Giving to charity through life insurance

Donating Assets

In exchange for donating assets (cash, stocks, bonds, or other property) directly to charity while you're alive, the government allows you to deduct the full value of the donated assets from your annual tax return. Though the immediate tax benefit may seem alarming, there are three reasons why outright gifting of assets may *not* be the best choice:

* You give up your ownership of the assets permanently.

* You no longer receive the benefits of holding the assets, such as dividend payments.

* You lose the prospect of allowing the assets to grow until you die

Charitable Trusts

Charitable trusts, generally called **charitable remainder trusts (CRTs),** offer grantors the option to donate assets to charity upon death *and* receive income and tax benefits during their lives. CRTs also help reduce the size of your taxable estate by shielding portions of your assets from future estate tax. CRTs have two types of beneficiaries:

Income beneficiaries: Receive income the trust generates during your lifetime or for a specified term

Death benefit beneficiaries: Receive the remainder of the trust following either the end of the trusts term or the death, of the income beneficiaries.

There are two main types of income-producing charitable trusts: **charitable remainder annuity trusts (CRATs)** and **charitable remainder unitrusts (CRUTs).** Each has its own advantages and disadvantages.

Though both CRUTs and CRATS are irrevocable, you can usually change the charity that is named as beneficiary at any time if your trust retains that right.

Tax Breaks and Benefits of Charitable Trusts

Both CRUTs and CRATs provide significant tax benefits.

Avoiding capital gains tax: The difference between what you paid for an asset (such as a stock) and its value upon sale-the **capital gain-is** not taxable if you place the asset in a CRUT or CRAT. Normally, the capital gain is subject to **capital gains tax** of 15-35%.

Avoiding estate tax: Because assets in the trust are out of your estate, they are not subject to estate taxes-yet you receive the income (which is taxable).

Getting tax deductions if you're subject to the alternative minimum tax:

Taxpayers can still receive tax deductions for assets given to charitable trusts even if they are subject to the alternative minimum tax (AMT). The AMT is a separate tax system that removes deductions and tax credits and forces taxpayers with many deductions to pay set minimum amounts of tax. Charitable contributions are one of the few deductions not currently eliminated for taxpayers subject to the AMT.

At minimum, a CRAT must distribute annually at least 5% of the initial fair market value of the trust at the time the CRAT is established. Fair market value means that the trust's assets must be valued as if they were to be *sold currently,* not at the value they had at the time they entered the trust. Federal law requires that 5% of this value then be paid to the income beneficiaries of the trust. CRUTs therefore must distribute annually at least 5% of the trust principal. Fair market value is the value on the date the trust is revalued, which happens annually.

Charitable Giving through Life Insurance

It's possible to designate a charity as the owner and beneficiary of insurance policies you hold. When you die, the charity receives the **death benefit-the lump** sum paid by the insurance company upon the policyholder's death. You can also give the charity the money required to pay the policy's premiums and in return you will receive an income tax break for that donation while you're still alive.

Charitable giving through life insurance may not be allowed in states that require beneficiaries to have an insurable **interest in your life-a** reason to want you alive rather than dead, such as a need for your income or care giving.

Donor Advised Funds

A donor-advised fund is a charitable giving vehicle administered by a third party and created for the purpose of managing charitable donations on behalf of an organization, family, or individual. A donor-advised fund offers the opportunity to create an easy-to establish, low cost, flexible vehicle for charitable giving as an alternative to direct giving or creating a private foundation. Donors enjoy administrative convenience, cost savings and tax advantages by conducting their grant making through the fund.

The following example is taken from Vanguard's marketing material for their plan:

Suppose you have 1,000 shares of stock that you purchased 15 years ago (thus, you're in long term capital gains territory). Assume that you purchased the stock for $10 per share and it is now worth $100 per share. Now, let's compare the cost to the donor of making a contribution of $100,000 to a charity of your choice. We assume a 35% income tax rate and 15% long-term capital gains tax rate.

Here are two simple examples:

Option 1: Contribute cash from sale of securities

> Immediate cost of donation: $100,000
>
> Capital gains tax incurred: $13,500 (15% times ($l00k minus $ 10k))
>
> Income tax saved: ($35,000) (35% times $100k)
>
> Net cost to donor: $78,500

Option 2: Contribute appreciated securities to donor advised fund

> Immediate cost of donation: $100,000
>
> Capital gains tax incurred: NA (15% times $100k minus $10k)
>
> Income tax saved: ($35,000) (35% times $100k)
>
> Net cost to donor: $65,000

Thus, you can effectively contribute $100,000 to the public charity of your choice for $13,500 less in actual donor cost by using the donor advised fund.

Chapter 6

Career Transition

The one constant in the life of a corporate executive is *change*! Transitions to new cities, new positions and new companies can impact corporate executives throughout their careers and it is important to manage assets and have everything under control during these changes. Here are some things to think about:

Leaving Your Job

* What would you like to do next?

* What about health and medical insurance?

* How do you continue an income stream?

* What to do with all retirement and stock options plans?

Distribution Strategies for 401k and Profit Sharing Plans

* Monthly annuity options

Usually includes monthly payments based upon age, marital status and account balance. Monthly annuity options can usually not be changed and are less advantageous for heirs.

* Direct rollovers into Individual Retirement Account

This is usually one of the best options, as there is no withholding tax, no 10% IRS penalty, and there continues to be the ability to defer income tax. A direct rollover is more beneficial for heirs and gives you the flexibility to have more options for your investments other than the investments offered through the plan.

* 60-day rollover

As long as you take receipt of the funds and rollover to a custodian IRA account or other qualified plan there is no 20% mandatory tax withholding.

* No rollover

If you decide to take receipt of the funds without rolling over to a qualified plan their will be a 20% Mandatory withholding to the IRS as well as potential ordinary income tax depending on your age and balance.

*   Leave money in current plan

In most cases you have the option to leave your retirement plan with the company plan without additional fees or charges and this may be a good choice if you are pleased with the current offering and do not have a better place to put your funds. Check with your plan administrator for this option.

*   Converting to a Roth IRA

Many employer plans can be converted to a Roth IRA and if so the income taxes are owed on the conversion, but the future IRA distributions are income taxis income tax free if taken after age 59 ½ ~ and five years from conversion. Adjusted gross income must be less than $100,000 to convert unless the limitation goes away in 2010 by a vote of government. This conversion is most beneficial if you have money outside of your IRA to pay the taxes, have at least a ten year time horizon and do not expect a big drop in tax bracket in retirement.

Net Unrealized Appreciation (NUA)

This is an option for company stock distribution out of a qualified plan, such as a 401 k, that allows the executive to convert unrealized appreciation on low cost basis stock into long-term capital gains. Typically, you would pay income tax on the average cost basis and not on the fair market value, and then pay capital gains on the additional stock only when sold. This will help to minimize taxes on employer stock portion of your retirement plan.

Exceptions to the 10% IRS Distribution Penalty

*   *   First Time homeowner
*   *   Qualified Education expenses
*   *   Death of IRA holder
*   *   Disability

* Medical expenses exceeding 7.5% of AGI

* Health Insurance after receiving unemployment for at least 12 weeks or more

* Substantially equal payments (Individuals under age 59 ~ and for five years)

Option Exercise

When it comes to leaving your company, it is very important to sit down or call the human resource director to find out what the status of your stock options will be. Each plan is different and some plans provide a payout on your current vesting schedule while other options may have forfeiture clauses. There are also many plans that accelerate your vesting schedule in the event of a merger or company buyout. If there is the ability to exercise your options please refer to the section on exercising stock options to figure out which is most beneficial for your financial situation.

Insurance Conversions Health Insurance Conversion

The Consolidated Omnibus Budget Reconciliation Act (COBRA) gives workers and their families who lose their health benefits the right to choose to continue group health benefits provided by their group health plan for limited periods of time under certain circumstances such as voluntary or involuntary job loss, reduction in the hours worked, transition between jobs, death, divorce, and other life events. Qualified individuals may be required to pay the entire premium for coverage up to 102 percent of the cost to the plan.

COBRA generally requires that group health plans sponsored by employers with 20 or more employees in the prior year offer employees and their families the opportunity for a temporary extension of health coverage (called continuation coverage) in certain instances where coverage under the plan would otherwise end.

Life Insurance

When your life insurance coverage ceases as a result of termination, you may have the right to convert some or all of your life coverage from the group plan to an individual plan. Evidence of your health will not be required to exercise this right of conversion.

Long- Term Disability Insurance

When your long-term disability coverage ceases as a result of termination, you may have the right to convert from the group plan to an individual plan. Other than a group disability, the only coverage for disability would be covered under social security on an individual disability plan purchased outside of the company.

Human Resources Department

The human resource department is your most important resource. Although there might be a lot of stress and concern in your life, make sure to treat these people as one of your team, as they can have a big impact on your ability to transition smoothly.

"Today knowledge has power. It controls access to opportunity and advancement."

Peter Drucker 1909-2005

About the Author

For 17 years, Chris Walling has been advising corporate executives and advisors about all aspects of investments and planning as well as hedging and monetization of publicly held stock. Chris is a founding partner and wealth advisor for a large independent investment firm in Columbus, Ohio, and has also previously worked as a Branch Manager and Financial Advisor with Smith Barney for 15 years in Cincinnati and Columbus, Ohio, as well as in the Seattle, Washington area. Chris has advised many corporate executives from Fortune 500 companies as well executives from technology and health care start up ventures.

Chris has been featured in Registered Representative Magazine for helping technology heavy investors on hedging through options, and has coached and trained many financial advisors on the basics of managing concentrated stock positions for corporate executives.

He lives with his family in Powell, Ohio.

www.ingramcontent.com/pod-product-compliance
Lightning Source LLC
Chambersburg PA
CBHW021041180526
45163CB00005B/2230

* 9 7 8 0 5 5 7 0 9 5 3 7 7 *